I0462331

50 Leadership Principles PART I:

How to position YOUrself for digital success

By Jorge Zuazola © founder of European Leadership © 12th July 2019

ISBN: 9781080346141

INDEX

4

PRINCIPLE #1: Digital Financial Freedom

Never leave a job until you find a new one. In the 4.0 Digital Economic Graph at LinkedIn you are able to secure several consulting roles to diversify your sources of income.

PRINCIPLE #2: Have what it takes

Success = Hard Work

To lead digitally all you need is a good leadership acronym, supported by a healthy LinkedIn Group as well as a web 2.0. The rest will follow suit

PRINCIPLE #3: Make Friends

Do not criticise, condemn or complaint.
Never ever engage in an argument with
anybody in the digital economic graph.

PRINCIPLE #4: Business Acumen

Often, people reject a digital business plan because they have a mental concept of what is supposedly like, or have heard from a second or third hand source or a disgruntled person. These people are losers who never venture out far enough into deep water to achieve success or attain the financial benefits they might have had. Taking the plunge in the digital business is just one of the simple risks in life.

PRINCIPLE #5: Your own digital route to prosperity

Do not take debt with credit cards, they are the enemy of prosperity

Do not live for the approval of others, specially when there is a new boss.

The route to prosperity starts with your own leadership concept.

PRINCIPLE #6: Think BIG

Ignore petty digital people, expect to be sniped at digitally, they are psychologically sick, feel sorry for populists, they are not as competent as you are. Greatness is an inside job.

PRINCIPLE #7: Speed of thought

Business will change in the next 5 years (2020 -2025) more than it has in the last 50 or even in the last 10.

PRINCIPLE #8: Financial intelligence

As the Digital Age continues its success you want to make sure that you have money working for you instead of you working for money

Keep in mind that the reason most people do not get wealthy in the Digital Era is because they have never been trained financially to see an opportunity which is right in front of them.

PRINCIPLE #9: Make your personality your ally

It does not matter whether you are both a Perfect Melancholic or a Powerful Choleric because it is the best mixture to succeed in the Digital World. As long as you do not enter into unnecessary arguments your leadership quality will always be appreciated by your digital community.

PRINCIPLE #10: Born to succeed

Success is about doing common things unusually well. One of the common things is self-talk which people ignore but is key to success. Do Self-Talk and record it on a daily basis. You will see amazing positive results sharing it with your 4.0 network. Your clients will flourish.

PRINCIPLE #11: Become unstoppable

With the 2008 recession, you may not have started life in the best of the circumstances but if you focus on something and keep on doing it you will succeed to become digitally unstoppable in a 4.0 networked world.

.

PRINCIPLE #12: Improve your digital communication skills

The golden rule of communication is:

Succinct and to the point.

As you can see in two simple lines or sentences you can communicate worldwide.

PRINCIPLE #13: Develop an Internet Strategy 4.0

The Internet is the revolution and we have to take advantage of it. Nowadays with social networks, either you are networked in or networked out. Put a strategy to have a large business network. Use the Internet conscientiously in the 4.0 IoT driven world.

PRINCIPLE #14: Digital Teamwork

Together

Everybody

Achieves

More

Life is teamwork. Teamwork is a key ingredient of success in business. In digitalization, this is even more important.

PRINCIPLE #15: Talk aloud digitally and grow up rich

Set money objectives and talk aloud about them with your digital network, do not procrastinate, take decisions.

PRINCIPLE #16: Enjoy your digital work

Whistle while doing your digital work, it is amazing what results you will get.

PRINCIPLE #17: Be an affirmer not an evaluator

Evaluators v Affirmers: One digital affirmer is worth 1000 digital evaluators. We have all, at one time or another in our lifetime, been crushed by an evaluator or two. Yet, particularly as believers, we are expected to appear victorious. We are expected to be on a continuous spiritual high. Our higher-self. We are animal spirits with intelligence. We are expected to fly, as the sparrows, undaunted into the storms of life.

PRINCIPLE #18: Plant seeds of greatness for your children

Children who grow up in the environments full of "putdowns", negative "nicknames", and criticism often become critical adults with less than adequate self-esteem in a 4.0 liquid world where everything is everywhere. Make sure that you use the language of success with your children in the 4.0 world as well.

PRINCIPLE #19: Be a digital winner

The winner is always part of the solution, the loser is always part of the problem. This is even truer nowadays in the digital world. Engage only on constructive leadership ideas and projects.

PRINCIPLE #20: Be a strategist at home

Most of the behaviour of the children is determined by the influence exercised on them during their first six years of live. Love your children at an early age and raise them up with the language of success in the Digital Age. Put a digital strategy at home before you put a strategy at work.

PRINCIPLE #21: Talk is not cheap

Bite your tongue until it bleeds specially when you talk to others. Be tougher when you speak to yourself i.e. send yourself a missile 'Cancel, Cancel' the thoughts from Lucifer trying to bring you down. This personal missile tells your brain to shoot down the negative digital message. It is your way of telling yourself not to store any negative message in your memory or let it harm your attitude.

PRINCIPLE #22: Digital Attitude is everything

Change your attitude and change your life. The sooner you realize you are source of inspiration for others, the faster you will become a leader

PRINCIPLE #23: Digital Smile Management

Wake up every morning with a WOW!, jumping out of your bed and thanking God for the privilege of living in the developed world. Go to the mirror, read your dreams and smile! Watch your favourite videos before you start working. Apply the Golden Hour reading at least 21 minutes before working. Smile Management applied in the Digital World will make wonders for you.

PRINCIPLE #24: Live your dream always

Guidelines for making your dream come true "I will do today as others will not, so I can live tomorrow as others cannot". Every single digital step you take puts you ahead of the game. Ahead of 99% of people.

PRINCIPLE #25: Be digitally skilled with people

Remember the first few seconds of any relationship usually sets the tone and the spirit of it (**before you break silence give people a sincere smile**). Harvard says that in the first 3 seconds an impression of you is made. Your LInkedIN profile transmits a first impression of you in just 8 seconds based on both your photo and your professional headline.

.

PRINCIPLE #26: Be an active digital networker

Being on the right track without taking action just means that you will get hit by the train. Networking 4.0 is exploding. You can take action and it will propel you. Or, you can do nothing and get blown away with the dust left by others who are passing you by.

.

PRINCIPLE #27: Be a digital magnet to people

Arouse in the other person an eager digital want. The mind does not get tired of reading positive inspiration.

.

PRINCIPLE #28: Turn job adversity into digital success

Foresight and faith can take you a long way toward changing your attitude about job adversity. Many of us have dreams and visions of what we would like our future to be. However, as long as they remain dreams and visions with no foundation in reality, there is very little chance of these dreams coming true. A dream without a plan is phantasy therefore in order to transform a wish into a reality you must begin to set your goals down in writing, and break them down into small, tangible steps that can be achieved in one giant digital leap.

PRINCIPLE #29: Success is one day at a time

Success is 99% failure (Sochiro Honda). This means that in digital terms as long as you work 1% correctly every day you will succeed.

PRINCIPLE #30: The digital mind will get you what you want

Protect your digital mind: it's a multimillion-dollar/euro/sterling/swiss franc/yen asset. Your mind is the exclusive source of all you will create spiritually and materialistically in your digital life. Your level of happiness, security, contributions to others, your dreams, all come from one place – your mind.

PRINCIPLE #31: Network digitally with your children

Children are constantly testing, attempting to see how much they can get away with, how far you will let them go, and they secretly hope you will not let them go too far with wrong digital habits. You have to network with them, to stop them as necessary. Ignoring them can prove costly over time.

PRINCIPLE #32: Become influential digitally

Apply the Law of Attitude which says that Enthusiasm is Contagious. This is even truer in the Digital Era

Thereafter apply the Law of Self-Confidence: The first 60 seconds of an encounter with a stranger are most lasting "Early impressions are hard to eradicate from the mind" – Jerome. A first good digital impression will pay-off for years to come.

PRINCIPLE #33: Listen for digital success

The next time you get into an argument with someone, stop the discussion for a moment, and for an experiment, institute the rule that each digital user can only answer for him or herself only after he/she has first restated the ideas and feelings of the other speaker accurately, and to that audience's satisfaction. Listening is the opposite of pressure. Listening leads to success. Listening is the fuel of progress in digital business. Pressure is like a brake in the fuel of digital growth.

PRINCIPLE #34: Be a leader in your heart

If God wanted us to talk more than listen, He would have given us two mouths rather than 2 ears. One of the key concepts in leadership is the 'Peter Principle': "People in organizations tend to rise to their level of incompetence". In other words, they keep getting promoted until they become a failure. The 2008 financial crisis evidenced that the Corporate World was an example of too much talk and application of the Peter Principle. You need to be a leader in your heart to keep going. You have to learn the basic leadership principle that when the going gets tough, the tough get going.

PRINCIPLE #35: Be intelligent with money

Intelligence solves problems and produces money. Money without financial intelligence is money soon gone. Most people fail to realize that in life, it is not how much money you make but it is how much you keep i.e. a 20% savings on your net annual income is a 20% bonus without paying tax. There are cases of lottery winners who are poor, then suddenly rich, then poor again or stories of professional athletes, who, at the age of 22, are earning millions a year and are sleeping under a bridge by the age of 36.

PRINCIPLE #36: Be a first-class time manager

In a 4.0 digital world as liquid as water, Corporate Executives finally realize that nowadays what happens on weekends and between 5 PM and 9 AM weekdays directly affects a person's performance from 9 AM to 5 PM. The person with a constructive off-the-job spiritual life nearly always is more successful than the person who lives in a dull, dreary home situation. You need a state-of-the art time management system. This is not negotiable i.e. each hour of your time should be divided in google calendar into green (100% productive) yellow (50%) and red (0%).

PRINCIPLE #37: Apply the word of mouth principle to your digital brand name

Jeff Bezos Founder and CEO of Amazon said in the 90s that word of mouth sharing accelerates online to an almost unfathomable degree...with the sole click of a mouse. Now in the 4.0 Digital World we all can tell that business recognizes the shift of power towards people. It is the P2P Digital Era for your success.

PRINCIPLE #38: Dream always otherwise you do not wake up

Always dream and shoot higher than you know you can reach. Don't bother just to be better than your contemporaries or predecessors in the Industrial Age, try to be better than yourself in the Digital Age". Without a vision you will stay at the level of mediocrity. Rather than allowing circumstances to affect you, you can take control. British Prime Minister Winston Churchill said "One ought never to turn one's back on a threatened danger and try to run away from it. If you do that you will double the danger. But if you meet it promptly and without flinching you will reduce the danger by half. Never run away from anything".

PRINCIPLE #39: Have confidence in dealing digitally with people

Speak up digitally with wise and inspirational words, people do not like those who mumble.

PRINCIPLE #40: Create wealth on the web through networking 4.0

Make a decision to start your dream business is certainly the first step toward living your dreams. The second step is to plan your life 5 years from now – your exit 4.0 strategy. You may want to cash in early. I certainly would sleep better if I knew my family and loved ones would be taken care of if something happened to me. Wouldn't you? Ask yourself "Is your income inheritable" by your children?

The world is literally at your fingertips today, and it has never been truer than with the Internet and Networking 4.0.

PRINCIPLE #41: Move out of comfort zone to seek for digital cheese

Old Industrial Age beliefs do not lead you to new Digital Age cheese. When you move beyond industrial fear, you feel free digitally. What would you do if you were not afraid digitally?": Some fear can be good. When you are afraid things are going to get worse if you do not do something, it can prompt you into action. But it is not good when you are so afraid that it keeps you from doing anything because the Law of Attraction is working. Move on while seeking your digital cheese.

PRINCIPLE #42: Self-talk is a digital leadership trait

The patterns of past experiences and feelings (both successes and failures) can be changed, somewhat as a digital recording may be changed by "dubbing in" new digital material or by replacing an old recording with a new one simply by recording over it. The patterns in the human brain tend to change slightly each time they are "played back" digitally. **In other words, we are not doomed or damned by the past. The old can be changed, modified, or substituted by our present positive digital thinking.**

PRINCIPLE #43: Be responsible for those you love is P2P Leadership

If you or, a loved one you are responsible for ends up in a nursing home, all the great things you wanted to do with your money, all the sums you eventually accumulate, all can be lost. Do not let this happen to you. There is nothing worse than seeing someone in his or her seventies or eighties devastated emotionally by losing a spouse to a nursing home, then also having to endure the financial devastation that can follow. Being responsible to those you love is knowing that you have taken care of everything, rather than just thinking that you have. Be responsible!

PRINCIPLE #44: Use a three-jar system for your finances

With the 2008 financial crisis adults who were serious about building long-term investment pipelines needed to start managing their money according to a three-jar system. But instead of putting their money into jars, they should put it into bank and brokerage accounts i.e.

1. Spend and Give for monthly expenses
2. Save for major expenses
3. Invest for pipelines.

PRINCIPLE #45: Believe and then anything is digitally possible

Without belief we would be left with nothing but an overwhelming doom, every single day. And it will beat you. We struggle daily against the slow lapping of ego driven cynicism. Dispiritedness and disappointment, these were the real perils of life, as they are ego driven.

Anything is possible. Make today count. You can be told you have a 90% chance of a 50% chance or a 1% percent chance, but you have to believe, and you have to fight. Be convinced beyond doubt that we are much better than we know. We have unrealised capacities that sometimes only emerge in crisis. Success is based on how you handle adversity.

PRINCIPLE #46: Become a digital prosumer

When you buy a Eur 100 item at 40% discount, you do not "save" Eur 40. You lose Eur 60! When you take Eur 60 from your net worth to buy a consumable, you not only lose the Eur 60, you lose the ability to invest that Eur 60 to create more money over time. That is why **consuming is such a drain on your net worth –takes away from, rather than adds to, your bottom line.** Would not it be great to "retire" from your job and enjoy financial freedom?... instead of retiring from your job at 65 and living off a small pension and Social Security. Set up your prosumer 4.0 network

PRINCIPLE #47: Manage yourself digitally from the inside out

In the journey from chaos to order, it is often easier to start with digital organizing, because it is much more tangible than time.

Because life moves so rapidly and changes so quickly, your Digital Time Plan ought to reflect your current goals, priorities, and interests. Every day and week, review your Digital Time Map. You may need to expand the time allotted for one activity, and shrink the time allotted for another.

PRINCIPLE #48: Be respectful of yourself and others

Leadership begins with how you feel about yourself,not what others say about you. Respect begins with knowing who you are, loving yourself, and accepting yourself. By leading digitally, you will beat

1.The fear of failure which keeps us from trying to succeed digitally.
2. The fear of losing which keeps us from trying to win digitally.
3. The fear of what everyone else will think which keep us from stepping out digitally.

PRINCIPLE #49: Become the CEO of your own digital company

In the Digital 4.0 World what you earn is directly proportional to what you learn. The will to win is important. But the will to win isn't worth a nickel unless you also have THE WILL TO PREPARE. For things to change, you have to change. When it is all said and done, you have a choice. You can continue to do things that will lead to frustration and unhappiness. Or you can make the changes that help you get what you want most out of life to start a new beginning. Many people COULD HAVE become a millionaire... or COULD HAVE become happier... or COULD HAVE become healthier... or COULD HAVE made a contribution —but didn't. Could haves and should haves get you nowhere. Start making the 4.0 changes you need to make TODAY...so that you can become the person you want to become TOMORROW!

PRINCIPLE #50: Bite your tongue until it bleeds

How come sometimes we feel defeated? The reason is the tongue driven by ego. Lucifer only has authority over us when we give him that authority with our mouth. This is the problem of 80% of the people. The essential implementing facts of the truly victorious life start on how to control our tongue above all in the digital world

Talk is not cheap. "What you say is what you get". The words of your mouth have control of your life, whether you like it or not, or whether you believe it or not. Avoid political and emotional tweets as well as irrelevant Facebook content. Be professionally digital at all times.

www.ingramcontent.com/pod-product-compliance
Lightning Source LLC
Chambersburg PA
CBHW051204170526
45158CB00005B/1807